Keys to the Past

Tudor Life and Dress

Series Editor: Edith Freeman

Edith Freeman, B.A.
Senior History Teacher,
Salters Hall School,
Sudbury, Suffolk.

Acknowledgements

The author wishes to thank Phillippa Glanville, Jackie Kramers, Sue Tibbetts and also the staff of the Suffolk Record Office, Bury St Edmunds, for their assistance. The Publishers acknowledge with thanks the co-operation of the Museum of London and the assistance of John Edwards, Barry Grey and Rosemary Weinstein.

The photographs on the title page and pages 28 and 29, 33 (right), 34 (bottom left) and 37 (bottom left) are reproduced by gracious permission of Her Majesty The Queen: copyright reserved.

Acknowledgements for other photographs are due to the following:

J. Allan Cash Ltd: 40 (top right); Army Photo: 6 (top right); Associated Press: 10 (top right); Bankfield Museum, Halifax: 22 (bottom), 23; BBC Hulton Picture Library: 42 (bottom left); Bodleian Library, Oxford: 45 (top right); British Library – from the Egerton MS. 1894, f.14: 5 (bottom left); Camera Press: 8 (bottom); Department of the Environment – Crown Copyright; 7 (top right); Everest Double Glazing: 40 (top left); T.M. Feldgate – photograph by G.F. Cordy from *Suffolk Heraldic Brasses* (East Anglian Magazine, Ipswich): 27; Fotomas Index: 4 (centre and bottom right), 5 (bottom right), 6 (bottom), 14 (bottom right), 42 (top), 44 (bottom left and centre), 45 (bottom), 46 (left and right), 47 (left); Nigel Heard – photograph by D.J. Floyd from *Wool: East Anglian Golden Fleece* (Terence Dalton, Lavenham, Suffolk): 43 (top); ILEA Learning Materials Service: 42 (centre); B.L. Kearley Ltd: 7 (bottom left); Keystone Press Agency Ltd: 6 (top left and centre), 8 (top); the Marquis of Bath, Longleat House: 40 (bottom); the Marquis of Salisbury, Hatfield House: 12 (top); Mary Evans Picture Library: 30 (top right), 31 (left), 38 (right), 39 (bottom left and right), inside back cover (bottom left); Massey-Ferguson: 44 (top right); National Portrait Gallery: 9 (left), 10 (bottom), 13 (left), 30 (bottom), 33 (left and right), 36 (bottom left), 38 (left), 39 (bottom left and bottom right), inside back cover (top, centre, bottom centre and bottom right); National Trust: inside front cover, 41 (left); Picturepoint London: 4 (top and bottom left), 44 (top left); Press Association: 10 (top left), 45 (top left); Private Collection: 3 (bottom); Ray Rathborne/*The Sunday Times*: 16 (right); Suffolk County Record Office, Ipswich – from *Portrait of a Tudor Worthy* by A. Daly Briscoe (East Anglian Magazine, Ipswich): 41 (right); Tate Gallery/John Webb: 21, 36 (top); Barrie Thorpe: 14 (centre); Victoria and Albert Museum – Crown Copyright: 7 (bottom right), 11 (top), 32, 35, 36 (bottom right); Viscount de L'Isle, V.C., K.G., from his collection at Penshurst Palace, Kent: 3 (top); Walker Art Gallery, Liverpool: 9 (right), 11 (bottom); Welsh Office: 43 (bottom).

Thanks are due to the Museum of London for the photographs on the following pages: 5 (top), 7 (top left), 12 (bottom), 13 (right), 15 (bottom left and bottom right), 18 (bottom), 19, 24 and 25, 31 (right), 34 (right), 36 (centre right), 37 (top), 39 (top), 48.

The following photographs have been provided by the Thomas Nelson Visual Resources Unit: page 26 (top) by Penni Bickle; pages 15 (top), 17, 18 (top), 20 (top and bottom), 22 (top and centre), 30 (top left), 36 (bottom centre) and cover by Chris Ridgers.

The costumes for the cover photograph have been supplied by BBC Television.

The transcript of Crown Copyright records in the Public Record Office on page 26 (bottom) appears by permission of the Controller of H.M. Stationery Office.

The Domesday Book entry on page 16 (left) appears by permission of the Public Record Office.

The picture of the sailor on page 47 (bottom right) is reproduced from *Handbook of English Costume in the Sixteenth Century* by C.W. and P. Cunnington (Faber and Faber).

Thanks are also due to the Science Museum, London, for permission to photograph two exhibits: 22 (top and centre).

Thomas Nelson and Sons Ltd
Nelson House   Mayfield Road
Walton-on-Thames   Surrey KT12 5PL
P.O. Box 18123   Nairobi   Kenya

116-D JTC Factory Building
Lorong 3   Geylang Square   Singapore 1438

Thomas Nelson Australia Pty Ltd
19-39 Jeffcott Street   West Melbourne   Victoria 3003

Nelson Canada Ltd
81 Curlew Drive   Don Mills   Ontario M3A 2R1

Thomas Nelson (Hong Kong) Ltd
Watson Estate   Block A   13 Floor
Watson Road   Causeway Bay   Hong Kong

Thomas Nelson (Nigeria) Ltd
8 Ilupeju Bypass   PMB 21303   Ikeja   Lagos

To study history you must become a detective

To develop your detective powers you will need to look carefully at the way we dress today and ask yourself why we choose the clothes we do. This will help you to discover why Tudor costume gives us a key to their very different way of life.

Look carefully at the picture below of a father, mother and three young boys. It was painted in 1568, early in the reign of Elizabeth I. What suggests they are inside a house? They are all wearing an article of clothing which is not generally worn indoors today.

The picture on the right shows a well-to-do Tudor mother and her six children, painted in 1596. What do you notice about the heads of most of the figures in this later painting?

Further on you will read about the alterations carried out in many Tudor homes during the reign of Elizabeth I: when you have learned

about them return to this page and suggest why there is something different about the heads of the two families.

In the 1596 painting two of the children are boys, although they are dressed more like women! What do you notice about the dresses of the elder girls compared with the costume of their mother?

Would you like to change clothes with these Tudor boys and girls? If not, why not?

Barbara Gamage and her children
▽

◁ Family portrait

Dressing for special activities

Adults and children in Tudor times enjoyed field sports, but there was not the variety of leisure pursuits in which we can take part. Nor would you have found shops selling sportswear!

The two boys pictured, bottom right, in a Tudor book on hunting are dressed to accompany adults in a day's sport. Do you think their costume is suitable for rough country?

Make a list of sports in which people take part today. Do not forget less common pursuits like pot-holing and hang-gliding. Collect pictures of sports clothes from magazines and catalogues. Discuss for what reasons different items in these outfits have been designed, e.g., to maintain a comfortable temperature? To enable your own side to pick you out? To help spectators to identify you? To look attractive? To protect you from injury?

The Tudor falconer pictured on the right has one item of clothing specially designed to protect him in his sport. Can you spot it?

◁ Tudor falconer

Tudor boys on a hunting trip
▽

4

On 17 January 1979, the BBC commentator on the Packer Cricket Match cried out in dismay when the Australian and West Indian teams came out dressed in canary yellow and bright pink. Why was he so shocked?

If you visit the Museum of London (or perhaps your local museum) you can see the article of protective clothing shown on the right. It is made of chain mail and was used in a favourite Tudor pastime, which trained men for more deadly activity. Can you guess what the sport was and why this article was worn?

Collect pictures of clothing worn today for protection.

Special forms of clothing for protection developed slowly in history. The fourteenth-century well-diggers in the picture below did not have much covering!

△
Tudor chain mail glove

◁ Medieval workmen

Tudor servant swatting flies
▽

The Tudor maid-servant swatting flies has a long coarse apron. Aprons were commonly worn by men, women and children at certain times of day. Why do you think Tudor people wore aprons so often?

Today you will find fewer people wearing aprons than in Tudor times but we have a much greater variety of 'protective clothing'.

Besides the items designed for use in sports, make a list of workers (like astronauts and road-workers) who wear 'protective clothing'. What kind of outfits do they wear and how well are they protected?

Why do you think that, in contrast to the Tudors, we have so many forms of protective clothing today?

5

The nation takes to uniform

When you cut out the pictures of clothing worn today for protection, did you find that any of them showed that the garments were part of a uniform?

Even the word 'uniform' (in the way that we use it to describe the costume worn by a soldier or sailor) did not exist before the middle of the eighteenth century. Now many people wear 'uniforms'.

List as many occupations as you can for which people wear uniforms. Why do you think they are necessary?

In the sixteenth century the nearest equivalents to uniforms were armour and 'liveries'. Liveries were special suits of clothes or badges worn by groups of men joined together to follow a common trade or maintained in the household of a great lord. English kings had tried to restrict the wearing of liveries. It led to 'gang war'. However, in the sixteenth century, new groups were allowed to wear them.

Elizabeth I with attendants
▽

Travelling troupes of players were almost as unpopular with Justices of the Peace as criminals. Often a drummer went ahead of the actors to attract a crowd in a town they were approaching. Queen Elizabeth I delighted in plays. Members of her household wore special livery like that shown in the picture. She gave permission to a company of actors to wear royal livery.

Why do you think travelling players were a nuisance? How would it help the Justices if the players wore a special livery? Write two paragraphs stating the case for and against wearing school uniform.

In Tudor times many of the soldiers who were recruited were given no special clothing. The gentleman in command would wear armour made specially for him. This steel helmet made in 1540 can be seen in the Museum of London. Try to find examples of pieces of Tudor armour in a museum in your area. Draw them.

The magnificent suit of armour pictured far right was made for Henry VIII and is on view in the Tower of London. Would you find it easy to fight in?

Can you suggest any other reasons besides protection why the King wanted such superb armour?

As cannon became more powerful, armour was of less and less value for protection. You can often find engravings of suits of armour on brasses in old churches. Try to find one of these engravings in your area. Borrow a book of pictures from your local library showing brasses. You will find Tudor armour was more decorative and impractical than it had been previously.

The picture below shows Henry VIII's ship the *Great Harry*. A sister ship, the *Mary Rose* was sunk at launching with all her crew and their sea chests. In 1980 archaeologists began a three-year operation to try to raise her. If they succeed you will be able to learn far more about what Tudor seamen chose to wear. Watch out for information.

△
Tudor helmet

Henry VIII's armour   ▷

Elizabethan armour   ▷

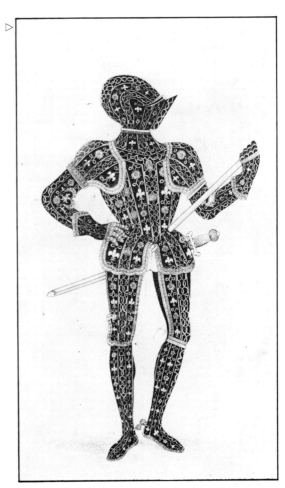

The *Great Harry*, 1520
▽

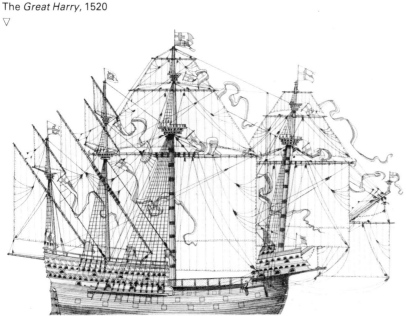

7

Cecil Beaton's coronation portrait of Elizabeth II ▽

Can costume increase authority?

On page 7 you were asked whether you could think of a special reason why Henry VIII had such a superb suit of shining armour made for him. It helped to give him *authority*.

Today those who follow certain professions dress in a certain way to instil respect. In the Courts of Law the judge and barristers wear complicated costumes which go back to Tudor times.

Can you think of other professions in which a special form of dress is worn to instil respect?

In our present-day society, respect for authority has declined. Sometimes those who wear special costumes become figures of fun. There are still head teachers who wear long black gowns and flat 'mortar boards' on their heads.

Do you think teachers would find it easier to keep order in a class if they wore a special costume?

The role of our monarch today is not an easy one. Queen Elizabeth II no longer governs the country as Queen Elizabeth I ruled England. Yet her experience is great. Find out how many prime ministers have held office since she became queen.

For many people she is still in a special sense the Head of the United Kingdom and of the Commonwealth.

Extravagant expenditure on her clothes might be resented by some of her subjects. It is said that, unlike Queen Elizabeth I, she is not fond of dressing up and prefers wearing a head scarf and tweeds. On state occasions, like the Opening of Parliament and during royal tours overseas, do you think it is important that her costume should give an impression of *majesty*?

In Tudor times it was not only the monarch who wore clothes to go with his or her position in life. Everyone (above thieves and vagrants) had *status*: a position demanding the fulfilment of responsibilities and commanding respect. Squire, parson, merchant, yeoman, craftsman, all had duties and expected recognition of their achievements. The laws forbade the wearing of certain garments, coloured fabrics and furs to those who were not entitled to them.

When Henry VII came to the throne in 1485 England had passed through a long period of strife, breaking out into civil war. Ordinary people longed for firm government to pursue their lives in peace.

Henry VIII and his daughter Elizabeth were both strong rulers and clever at finding ways to impress their subjects.

Look at the portrait of Henry VIII. His splendid costumes increased his natural ability to command. It needed heroic courage to defy him. Can you think of anyone, perhaps a member of staff at school, who easily commands obedience?

Queen Elizabeth I also made use of gorgeous clothes to make a greater impression. Do you think her subjects would have worshipped her as they did if she had not dressed up so magnificently to fulfil the role of queen?

△
Holbein the Younger's
portrait of Henry VIII

◁ The coronation portrait of
Elizabeth I

9

A queen cannot choose clothes just to please herself

Elizabeth I dressed in the French style

▽

The creation of outfits for Queen Elizabeth II is a challenge to designers. Not only must the Queen give an impression of majesty, she must be sensitive to the feelings and customs of the people she visits. As the guest of the Pope she wore a long-sleeved black gown. Among the Fiji islanders she was dressed in bright, floral prints. She must not offend taste by being too extreme.

It is not easy to steer between the dull and adventurous. She has to wear a hat which shows her smile and colours which the crowd can see at a distance.

Her clothes must be practical. In the outfit pictured here the designers made a mistake. Up flew her skirts in the wind!

Cut out and collect pictures of the Queen performing different engagements. Suggest an outfit which you think would be suitable for opening a school or hospital.

Compare the manner in which Queen Elizabeth I dressed with that of Elizabeth II.

In 1577 the King of Spain's half-brother received an envoy from Elizabeth who brought a miniature painting of her. Don John was 'moche pleased' and asked if Elizabeth dressed in the Spanish manner. The reply was, 'in diverse attires, Italian, Spanish, French as occasion served.' Don John begged for a portrait of the Queen dressed in the Spanish manner. Fifteen years earlier a Scottish visitor recorded that, on successive days, the Queen wore the dresses of different nations.

Borrow a book from the library showing pictures of Queen Elizabeth I. Roy Strong's *Portraits of Queen Elizabeth I* is the most complete. Select your favourite costume.

The picture on the left shows Elizabeth I in 1592. Why do you think she was not dressed in the Spanish style in that year?

10

A young woman of Elizabeth's Court

The description of the wool and cloth trade later in this book will show you how important it was that the people of England should be interested in clothes. It was fortunate that their Queen, Elizabeth I, needed no prompting to interest her in dress. As a child, she was kept so short of money that sometimes her underwear was scarcely decent. Are you surprised that when she became Queen she wanted to look wonderful?

There is a story which shows her later love of fine clothes. It also reveals one of those little weaknesses of character which made her people love her: one of her ladies appeared at Court in a lovely new gown. The Queen eyed it with envy. She asked if she might try it on. Soon Elizabeth appeared wearing the gown and looking ridiculous because the skirt was much too short. Thankfully, the lady remarked that Her Majesty could not wear the dress as it did not suit her. 'No', replied the Queen sharply, 'and it does not suit you, so you cannot wear it either!'

Using the picture which shows Queen Elizabeth I looking envious and sour and that of the lady-in-waiting in the pretty gown, try retelling the story in your own words and illustrating it.

There is another true story which shows Elizabeth I's passion for clothes: when she died, her wardrobes were opened and about 2,000 outfits were found. She never threw away even a stocking. Queen Anne, the wife of James I, who succeeded Elizabeth, was not so thrifty. She ordered her maids to cut up the beautiful gowns to make costumes for an entertainment!

Hilliard's portrait of Elizabeth I

Glitter and pageantry

Queen Elizabeth's love of clothes was matched by her pleasure in jewels. Her subjects shared this passion. Not only were jewels loved as ornaments by the Tudors, they were a means of storing wealth; it was believed they could cure sickness and work magic!

Below are pictured five items found buried at Cheapside, in the City of London, and now on view with other jewels in the Museum of London. It is believed that the hoard was buried by a goldsmith during an outbreak of plague early in James I's reign.

Can you place these labels against the correct item?

1 A hair ornament (amethyst drops and gold).
2 A shepherd's crook hairpin, set with rubies.
3 An enamelled pendant (how many ways can you think of wearing it?)
4 A toadstone (highly polished, fossilised fish tooth).
5 An amethyst hat badge.

Which one do you think was believed to work magic?

△
The *Ermine Portrait* of Elizabeth I

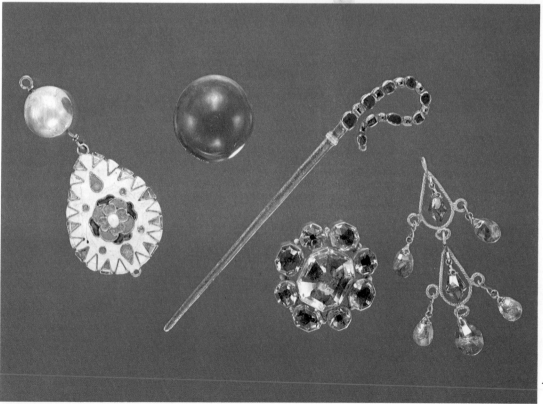

◁ Items from the Cheapside Hoard

Both Henry VIII and Elizabeth I had a sense of pageantry. The Tudor Court – the life of those who surrounded the monarch – became more dazzling than at any time in English history.

Men's costumes were even more extravagant than women's clothes. If the cloak with which Sir Walter Raleigh bridged the puddle for Queen Elizabeth was as fine as the one he has slung over his shoulder in this picture, he was certainly a very gallant courtier. Remember there were no dry cleaners or washing machines in Tudor times!

Alas, few of these gorgeous garments have survived. Most Tudors wore their clothes for years and then bequeathed them by will to others. Wills are one of our most important sources of information about Tudor clothes.

Try to find out if there are any Tudor wills in your county record office.

Fortunately, in the Museum of London, you can see the handsome blue satin cloak embroidered with gold thread which is pictured below. You will also find examples of magnificent men's gloves with embroidered tops. These have survived because they were carried for show, not worn. Design a coloured pattern for the top of a pair of gloves for yourself.

In part, the passion of the people of Tudor England for dressing up was inspired by the Court. Today, the strongest interest of the majority of English people seems to be sport. Can you suggest the reason for this obsession with sport?

Sir Walter Raleigh
▽

Gentleman's cloak, hat and gloves
▽

Are clothes a clue to position and wealth?

Look at the children playing in a park, the people coming out of a building like a bank, or the crowd leaving some sporting event. Can you be sure from the clothes they are wearing whether they come from wealthy families, or what kind of job they or their parents have?

Clothes today do not indicate social class and prestige as much as they did in Tudor times. Why?

Towards the end of the last century a revolution in production began which made much cheaper fabrics available. First rayon was made from cellulose, a substance present in all plant life. In 1934 an even greater revolution took place. Nylon was discovered as a by-product of petrol refining. There followed a whole range of what we call synthetic fabrics, manufactured by chemical processes. In addition, more and more garments were mass-produced and sold 'off-the-peg' in chain stores. The fashion creations of famous designers were quickly copied.

Make a list of all the garments you wear, noting from the labels inside the fabrics from which they are made.

A mass-produced anorak made of synthetic fibre
▽

The clothes the Tudors wore usually revealed their status in society. For example, in the early sixteenth century a certain shade of blue was used for servants and apprentices. Wealthy ladies and gentlemen could buy expensive, imported fabrics like velvet, satin, damask, taffeta. Most of the population had to make do with much coarser kinds of material.

The Elizabethan beggars in the picture below are well-covered and well-shod. Tudor clothes usually gave a clue to a person's wealth and occupation but overall the nation was probably better clothed than at any period in history. Why were the people of sixteenth century England so well clothed?

Do you know the area shown in the map below?
Find it on a map of England.

For more than three centuries, trade and industry based on a particular raw material had been building up the wealth of the nation.

Turn to the inside front cover of this book. The picture of Lavenham Guild Hall shows you the meeting place of the merchants engaged in the activities which had made England rich. On the facing page is the church of Long Melford, a mini-cathedral, one of the many splendid churches which the people of Suffolk could afford to build. Have you guessed the trade which was so prosperous, particularly in East Anglia and the Cotswolds?

The major wool and cloth area in Tudor England
▽

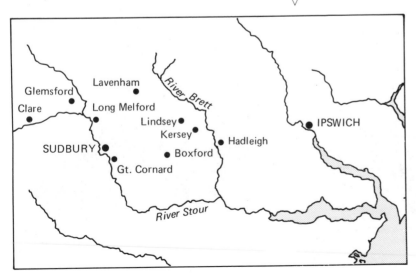

Tudor beggars
▽

The national wealth was not equally shared among the people. Fortunately the natural resources, which made it possible to be warmly clad and well shod, were easily available in most localities. Even those with tiny incomes could provide themselves with cloth and leather.

Plough-oxen, deer and other animals supplied hides. The number of surviving shoes and remnants of shoes, hand-made and so more comfortable, suggests few went barefoot.

Even if the local product was coarse, the majority of the people of England were dressed in wool. The woollen 'leg-wear', below right, which you can see in the Museum of London, may not be elegant but it was warm.

What are the advantages and disadvantages of garments made from synthetic fabrics compared with those made from wool?

△
Long Melford Church,
Suffolk

Tudor shoes
▽

Tudor stockings
▽

Sheep and the English wool and cloth trade

To understand the importance of dress in Tudor life it is necessary to look back further into the history of our nation; to follow the development of the wool and cloth trade and understand why sheep had become the foundation of the English economy.

The English climate and soils suited sheep. The Saxons probably valued the animals most as mobile manure-spreaders. They were penned on fallow ploughland: then the simple enclosure was moved to enrich another plot. They also provided wool, skins, meat and milk. By the time the Normans conquered England, the importance of sheep was firmly established. This is shown both in place-names and in the 'Domesday Book', produced for William I in 1086 as the great record of his conquered Kingdom. Below, in clerk's Latin, is the entry for Sudbury, Suffolk.

The entry tells us that on the Lord's demesne, there were two horses, seventeen plough-oxen, twenty-four swine and a hundred sheep.

By the twelfth century, wool had become England's leading export. Much of the trade was carried on by foreigners. They bought up English raw wool and transported it to the continent, where it was made up into cloth. Then they reimported the finished product to sell in England. Only the wealthy could afford these imports; the peasants wove rough cloth locally. Gradually English merchants took over the export of the raw wool, while better quality cloth was developed at home. This demanded both greater skills in spinning and weaving and also improvements in sheep-breeding.

The ram shown in the picture below is one of the rare remaining descendants of an important breed of Tudor sheep known as 'Norfolk Horns'. You can see specimens at Whipsnade Zoo in Bedfordshire. Try to find flocks of sheep in your area and notice how they differ from each other and from Tudor sheep. Do you know any place-names suggestive of sheep, like Sheepwash, Northumberland?

Between 1348 and 1349 the *Black Death* wiped out about a third of the people of England. The result was that workers were able to demand higher wages, and much abandoned land was available to be bought cheaply. Landowners began to keep sheep permanently on pasture instead of penning them on ploughland. The quality of wool was improved. Experiments in crossing various breeds of sheep produced both better results and greater variety. By the close of the fourteenth century, fifty-one grades of wool were available.

The Domesday Book entry for Sudbury, Suffolk
▽

The Norfolk horn ram: a rare descendant of the Tudor breed
▽

The opportunity to use better wool improved the performance of English spinners and weavers. To stimulate this success, King Edward III encouraged highly-skilled Flemish craftsmen to settle in England. The splendid fourteenth-century home and workplace shown below belonged to one of these immigrant weavers who settled in Kersey, Suffolk.

The demand for wool increased. By the time the first Tudor King, Henry VII, came to the throne in 1485, the land freed by the depopulation of the Black Death had all been taken up. Grasping landowners enclosed common and waste land, on which their poorer neighbours had depended for feeding their few animals and for gathering fuel, for their own sheep. The stronger, more ambitious landowners persuaded, or forced, the rest of the community to swap strips in the old open fields, so that these formed a single holding. The poor were often cheated and could not afford to fence their new plots. Large landowners enclosed their great estates, chiefly to pasture sheep. One Norfolk landowner's flock numbered 15,000. Everywhere was heard the cry, 'Sheep eat up men'.

◁ A Flemish weaver's house in Kersey, Suffolk

Tudor governments faced a choice as awkward as governments today. To improve the health of the nation twentieth-century governments wish to discourage smoking, but the government receives a large sum of money from a tax on tobacco. Sixteenth-century governments were alarmed by the social unrest in the countryside and the swarm of beggars who drifted into London. They introduced regulations to check the enclosure of land for sheep pasture. On the other hand, the nation's prosperity depended on the wool and cloth trade.

As cloth manufacture had improved in England the export of raw wool had declined. In 1350, 30,000 sacks were exported; in 1600, only 150 sacks. This did not matter when home sales and export of finished cloth increased.

In the early part of the sixteenth century, the sale of English cloth abroad trebled. Then in the middle of the century, troubles on the continent almost closed our markets abroad.

Elizabeth I's government tried to encourage home sales of English woollens. In 1571, the *Statute of Caps Act* ordered all those under the rank of gentleman to wear an English woollen cap on Sundays and holidays.

The woollen cap pictured below can be seen in the Museum of London. You can also see another of these caps in the Museum at Norwich. Would you like to have to wear such a cap?

H.M.Govt. Health Depts'. WARNING: CIGARETTES CAN SERIOUSLY DAMAGE YOUR HEALTH
LOW TAR

The Tudors found these woollen caps convenient for work but were ashamed to be seen in them on social occasions and festivals. Do you have any clothes you do not like wearing?

Queen Elizabeth I was not prepared to apply this 'wear wool campaign' to herself. She continued to import costly silk garments. However, she encouraged the improvement of the home manufacture of wool stockings for her subjects. After the introduction of a knitting frame in 1589, this industry became very prosperous.

Look back at the story told on page 11 of the Queen's behaviour towards one of her court ladies who appeared in a dress more attractive than her own. Had it been possible, Elizabeth I might have ordered all the ladies at the Court to wear home-spun woollen gowns. Queen Elizabeth I did banish more than one of her maids-of-honour from Court for daring to marry without royal permission but there were limits even to her authority!

A knitted cap for the lower orders
▽

The Queen's attitude to her male courtiers was very different. Her admirers were expected on all occasions to be splendidly dressed. She never forgave her favourite, the Earl of Essex, for forcing his way into her dressing-room in mud-spattered garments, even though he did cover her hands with kisses. The boldest courtier would not have dared to enter her presence in a woollen cap. She had a sharp eye for such fashions as the elegant gentleman's hat pictured below. It is handsomely trimmed with rich imported velvet.

Do you think people should be encouraged to buy home-produced goods? Would you buy a British car if a more desirable foreign model was available?

A smart gentleman's hat
▽

Again and again England's cloth trade has been saved by the combination of the skill of her inventors, the patience of her sheep-breeders and the adaptability of her clothiers. As early as the thirteenth century there are records of a special type of cloth woven from the fleece of sheep but differing from the traditional woollens. This *worsted* cloth had certain advantages: the surface was smoother; the edges frayed less; it was very long-lasting.

Wool with a long staple was required to weave worsteds. You will read in the account of spinning how the wool fibres were prepared in a different way.

At first, English worsteds found few buyers abroad but as their special qualities became known, demand for them grew. Clever foreign merchants began to buy up the long staple wool from the English sheep. This was manufactured on the continent into finer worsteds than the English had created. These fabrics were then exported to England. The English manufacturers were indignant. They despised these light materials as mere 'fripperies', but the eagerness of fashion-conscious English society forced them to produce more refined products themselves. Elizabeth I showed foresight by encouraging Dutch refugees, skilled in the new creations, to settle in East Anglia. You can find reminders of these Dutch immigrants in surnames, and in the influence on building styles.

Tufts of wool showing different lengths of staple ▷

Look at the roofs of the houses pictured below in Sudbury, Suffolk where Dutch weavers settled. Contrast the high-pitched roof of the timbered house on the right with the roofs on the left.

Can you discover any surnames which are Dutch in origin?

Where the settlers were few in number they were accepted by the local community. When a whole colony of Dutch weavers was established, as in Colchester, Essex, there was bitter hostility which led to riots. Can you think of any other examples of newcomers being made acceptable to an old-established community?

Gradually, the English clothiers recognised how much they could learn from the immigrants: they responded to the challenge by improving on their skills.

◁ Contrasting roofs, showing Dutch influence, in Sudbury, Suffolk

The picture below shows an elaborately-dressed young woman in 1569. Until the new worsteds were perfected, only Elizabeth I's richest subjects could have afforded such glamorous garments. Finer wool of long staple, either alone or mixed with other fibres, could be made to look like silks, satins and velvets. The clothiers even conjured up poetic names for these new creations: *Pearls of Beauty* was an imitation of a costly oriental fabric of silk and camel's hair.

Sateens was a type of worsted, cunningly made with a finish like the shine of satin. *Pyramids* was a very fine worsted which incorporated different coloured threads.

At last, all but the very poorest could appear on festival days, dressed almost like royalty. That such a miracle could happen was the result of technical advances illustrated on the next pages.

◁ A young lady, 1569

The improvement in the production of woollen thread in the Tudor period is important when you remember how little the process of spinning had changed in thousands of years.

The crude wool shorn from the fleece was prepared for weaving woollen cloth by carding. This involved brushing the fibres of the raw wool between two spiked boards.

The simple spinning implement still in use in most homes in early Tudor times was little more than a stick of hard wood 8 inches to 12 inches long.

It was found that fibres pulled from a bundle of raw wool could be transformed into thread by twisting them together. Even better, a short stick, dangling from one hand, could be set to spin with the other hand. If a few fibres were attached to the spinning stick, they could be twisted into yarn. Experiment showed that if the stick was inserted through a small circular weight the spinning of the stick became faster and steadier and the fibres formed a stronger thread.

Try experimenting yourself. You can even spin with a pencil and a circle of cardboard!

Few early spindles survive. They were probably burned. However, many whorls of pottery, stone, metal, bone and even wood have been found. You can see examples of whorls in museums throughout the country.

Feeding the loose fibres of raw wool on to the spindle was made easier by the use of a distaff. This was not unlike a broomstick handle to which a bundle of carded raw wool was attached. The pole might be tucked under one arm or stuck in the floor.

Loose yarn produced in this simple manner could be used to weave woollens. Worsteds demanded a firmer, more even thread with a higher twist.

Longer staple wool, with the fibres combed parallel with a strong metal comb instead of the carding operation, produced a yarn satisfactory for the coarse worsteds. It was still not possible to provide a thread which was strong, fine and even enough for the 'new draperies'.

△
Carding the crude wool

△
A whorl

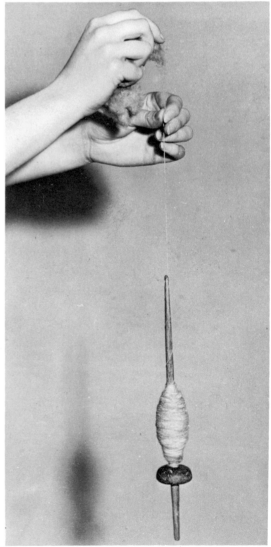

A spindle to which ▷
carded
wool is being fed

Demand stimulated invention and craftsmanship. Experiments in attaching a wheel to turn the spindle had been tried and used by some spinners. The technique was greatly improved in the late sixteenth century. The photograph shows a Tudor spinning wheel in the Museum of Halifax. It is an adaptation of the early sixteenth century hand implements. The spindle is turned by the wheel. This model is hand-rotated; later models were worked by a foot-treadle. The rotation of the spindle was speeded up and steadied as the machines improved. In most models the distaff was attached to the frame, as shown in the picture. In some models, however, it was spiked into the ground. With the great improvement in the quality of thread achieved by use of the better spinning wheels, the needs of the manufacturers of the 'new draperies' could be met.

A Tudor spinning wheel
▽

The Cheapside hoard

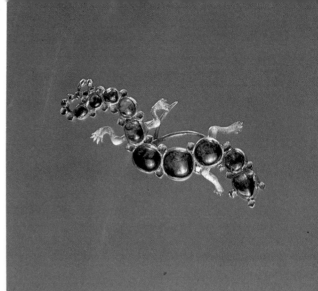

How fast do fashions change?

Fashions have never changed as fast as they change today. Study a queue of people, taking care not to give offence. Make sketches and notes on what they are wearing, paying special attention to footwear and headgear. Compare your observations with those of your friends.

Do you try to keep up with the latest fashion trends?

There were two special inspirations for new fashions in clothes in the sixteenth century.

From the reign of Henry VIII it became the custom for young noblemen to travel abroad. They were fascinated by the costumes of those in other European countries. They returned with numerous garments bought on their tours, eager to show off their new finery.

In 1558, a pretty young princess became Queen of England. Look back at her coronation portrait on page 9. Note that she developed her father's interest in clothes. Reread the story on page 11, where you will discover how many outfits she collected in her wardrobe during her lifetime. Queen Elizabeth's delight in dressing up infected her subjects.

The literature and paintings of Tudor England suggest that they were more obsessed with dress in that period of history than we are today.

In spite of this keen interest in clothes and the spurs to experiment in new styles, changes in fashion were much slower than they are today. As you read this page and the two which follow, note down the reasons why most of the Tudor population did not change their outfits as often as we do. Further on in this book you will find more important reasons why certain ways of dressing remained constant for the whole population throughout the Tudor period.

The young Elizabeth I at her accession to the throne
▽

Do clothes get passed on from one member of your family to another?

Count the number of children in the Tudor family in the picture below. Large families were frequent. It was hard luck on the last baby to whom a well-worn Tudor garment was passed down. For how many years might an article of clothing be worn if it were passed from girl to girl in the Tudor family pictured?

You may buy some of your garments from jumble sales or Oxfam shops, but today clothes which have years of wear in them are often discarded because fashions change.

Clothes would not have been discarded in the sixteenth century. Think about how Queen Elizabeth I hoarded hers. When the rich were willing to give away garments they were eagerly sought after by poor friends and relations or servants.

Edward Duke and his family
▽

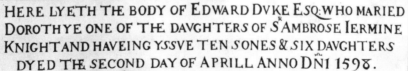

HERE LYETH THE BODY OF EDWARD DVKE ESQ: WHO MARIED DOROTHYE ONE OF THE DAVGHTERS OF Sᴿ AMBROSE IERMINE KNIGHT AND HAVEING YSSVE TEN SONES & SIX DAVGHTERS DYED THE SECOND DAY OF APRILL ANNO DÑI 1598.

Clothes were precious possessions

When Henry VIII closed the Priory at Montacute, Somerset, in 1539, a handsome pension was awarded to the former prior, Robert of Sherbourne. In his will, Robert made a list of his possessions, including all his gowns and even his spoons and glasses. Ask your local record office to show you a copy of the will of a Tudor person with a comfortable income. Note how many items are articles of clothing.

Make a list of all the articles you own. You will probably find that already you possess far more than the average adult in Tudor times.

How highly do you value your clothes among your possessions? Which possessions matter most to you?

Good material in a garment was much too precious to waste. After long wear it was usually reduced to smaller and smaller garments.

A will of 1559 says, 'also I give one shorte gowne to make a cote . . .'.

We read that in 1519, 'my scarlet gaberdine was bequeathed to make her a kirtle'.

Garments cut smaller and smaller ended up as household cloths or nose-wipers. Handkerchiefs were for show only. You blew into a piece of old cloth like the *muckinders* you can find in a case at the Museum of London.

The Field of the Cloth of Gold
▽

It was only the high-born or the ambitious courtiers, and the vain townsmen with fortunes made in trade, who followed the extremes of fashion. Below is the famous painting of the meeting of Henry VIII and the King of France, known as *The Field of the Cloth of Gold*. Even those who wore gorgeous outfits to accompany the King were probably not sorry to slip back into a warm, old gown when they returned home to the chills of England.

The less well-to-do Tudors were as eager to find out about changes in styles of dress as we are to know the football results today. They made attempts to imitate new fashions which were resented by those of higher rank.

There is a story of a Suffolk gentleman who was much vexed by a tradesman who attempted to copy his new clothes. The gentleman had his own sleeves slashed more and more finely. Finally, in trying to make the slits in his own sleeves even closer together, the tradesman cut the cloth to ribbons!

The restrictions on the wearing of certain apparel which the well-born and wealthy tried to enforce on those beneath them were reinforced by government regulations. The attempt to impose differences in dress to mark social position might have been more resented but for the English sense of humour.

Here is the satirical Tudor description of a young gallant returned from his travels, decked out in all the garments he has acquired:
French doublet,
German hose,
Italian ruff
And Flemish shoes.
Spanish cloak,
Venetian stuff –
Why all that's English
Is his NOSE!
This walking geography of clothes.

What were the most popular Tudor garments?

Nowadays, we often skimp materials and wear the minimum of garments.

There are various reasons why the Tudors used so much more material to make their clothes than we do today. The story of the wool trade should have given you one clue. Other reasons will become clear as you read on.

Tudor lady wearing a voluminous gown　▷

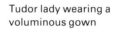

If you study brasses and tombstone figures in churches you will see that throughout the whole period the most popular garment for men, women and children was the gown. The gown was voluminous, in other words large and loose. It was not uncommon to use twelve yards of material for a gown, like that of the lady pictured top right who lived in the reign of Henry VIII. (A yard = 0.9 metre.)

Can you guess who the figure pictured below right is? In the reign of Henry VIII, with the exception of the King, he was the most powerful man in England. His gown, of enormous amplitude, sets off his power.

Copy the two gowns pictured and colour them.

Can you calculate how much material was needed to make your top garments?

Turn back to page 27. You will see that almost at the end of the long reign of Elizabeth I, a gentleman and his wife are still shown dressed in gowns. Most fashionable people about town would no longer be dressed in gowns in Queen Elizabeth's time when they appeared in public, but they probably would be glad to slip back into them when they returned to their country houses. The elderly, and those in certain professions, continued to wear gowns, even in public, throughout the Tudor period.

CARDINAL WOLSEY

Copy the drawing of an elderly divine and a statesman.

If you visit the National Portrait Gallery in London or Montacute House in Somerset, try to see the paintings of Tudor people.

The picture below right shows a beautifully embroidered nightgown which can be seen in the Museum of London. It probably survived because it was designed for a wedding night and was folded away in lavender afterwards.

Many Tudor people never undressed. Others slept naked but wore a warm loose wrapper in the bed-chamber or for comfort in the evening. The word 'nightgown' usually applies to this loose garment which was worn by both men and women and was often lined. In 1555, a man's nightgown is described as being 'of black satten furred with sables'.

All the gowns have a common characteristic. They are large and loose. As you read on you will understand why.

◁ Divine, middle sixteenth century, and statesman, late sixteenth century

Tudor nightgown
▽

The long gown was not a dashing garment. In the reign of Henry VIII most young men about town wore it shortened. The gallant courtiers who buzzed around the dazzling Queen Elizabeth wore hip-length, eye-catching cloaks.

Fortunately, the manufacture of leg-wear had much improved. Men proud of their calves, like the fashionable young man pictured here, dreaming among the roses, wore 'whole hose' (breeches and stockings in one piece). More common wear for men of fashion was upper hose (breeches) with separate stockings.

The picture on the facing page shows the Earl of Leicester's 'egg-timer' waist. From the middle of Queen Elizabeth I's reign, trunk-hose began to swell out like bells. They grew increasingly baggy, gradually losing their bell-shape, and became known as 'slops'. These were worn by sailors, workmen and those without such shapely legs.

These enormous 'bags' were not as foolish as might appear. Have you ever tested the temperature inside a snowdrop bell? It is several degrees higher than the outer air, thus protecting the vital parts of the flower.

Most fashionable men, if they wore 'slops', liked to have them stuffed. They used wool, rags and bran. There is even a story of a Suffolk gentleman who had his bed cut up and carried it around in his trunk hose! Whether this was due to shortage of stuffing, or to obtain a cheap lodging in London when he had to attend Parliament, is not known, nor whether the bed was a four-poster!

The story of the bed may be exaggerated, but we do know that special scaffolding had to be set up in the chamber where Parliament met, to enable the men who had vast breeches to squat.

Could you carry even a sleeping-bag in your jeans?

△
An elegant courtier,
c.1588

◁ The Earl of Leicester

Elizabeth I wearing a
French-style farthingale
▽

As the trunk-hose of men grew wider, so did women's skirts. Throughout the first half of the century the dress of women was slowly changing. For many, the kirtle, a simple garment worn under the gown, became the top garment. Then the kirtle split into a separate bodice and skirt. As the skirt gained importance it was divided in front to reveal an embroidered underskirt.

Whereas special arrangements were made to accommodate men's breeches, no such favour was shown to women as their skirts grew wider. It must have been very difficult to sit down, and some doors were too narrow for a woman to enter.

The young Queen Elizabeth I led the nation in adopting more and more voluminous skirts. Her ladies at Court eagerly followed the extravagant example of French and Spanish women. The new style was known

as 'the farthingale.' A frame was made of whalebone, wire, wood, or even rushes for the less wealthy. Hoops of wider and wider circumference were set from waist to toe tips. The skirt and underskirt were spread over these huge frames. The French farthingale which the Queen is wearing in the picture was tub-shaped. The Spanish farthingale was bell-shaped, the skirt being split to show the underskirt.

In 1599, a popular playwright wrote this rhyme:

Alas, poor farthingales
Must lie in the street.
To house them no door
In the city, made meet.

Can you suggest any practical reasons for wearing these voluminous skirts to outweigh the disadvantages?

Layer upon layer

Sixteenth century women would wear a number of layers of clothing. The picture below helps to show how many layers of clothing could be accommodated. Women wore shirt-shape chemises next to the skin. A specially fine, linen specimen embroidered in pink silk can be seen in the Museum of London and is pictured below right.

Over the chemise came petticoats: over these there was often a kirtle topped by the gown. Later the kirtle was frequently worn as the top-garment. By the middle of the sixteenth century most kirtles were divided into separate bodices and skirts. The skirt was often open to show the embroidery on an underskirt or false front. The picture on the previous page showed how the skirt swelled into the farthingale. A waistcoat might be pulled on over the bodice in chill weather. Those women who had abandoned the long gown might pull on a loose overgown in cold rooms and outside, covering this with a long cloak or gaberdine. For travel, there was a further 'safeguard' over the skirt and, in a coach, a lap-mantle around the knees.

Women's legs were less exposed than those of men. Nonetheless, they would often wear two pairs of stockings at once: 'nether stockings of worsted and next her legs a payre of hose or white jersey', writes a Tudor correspondent.

◁ Cecily Heron in summer attire, c.1527

Embroidered linen chemise
▽

The costume worn by Tudor men also allowed the wearing of layer upon layer.

From the reign of Henry VII all but the very poor wore a linen shirt next to the skin. You can see the fine example, pictured below, in the Victoria and Albert Museum.

Next might come a waistcoat or under doublet; fitting close over this a doublet. If a furred, long gown topped this it might be sufficient even for winter.

In the reign of Henry VIII, a courtier usually wore a jerkin or jacket over the doublet with a wide 'U' opening to the waist. Over this was slung a short gown. In the reign of Elizabeth I a circular cloak (see page 13) replaced the short gown.

Combinations of these garments varied. In the country a simpler, warmer 'cassock' might replace the jerkin and doublet. Labourers usually wore a loose coat of varying length as a top-garment.

When men's legs became more exposed (see page 32) as the gown shortened or was replaced by the circular cloak, they compensated, on cold days, by wearing stockings in duplicate or triplicate.

A character in a play of 1599 declares, 'two pairs of silk stockings that I put on, being somewhat a raw morning, one peache and another . . .', Try such mixtures, they produce interesting colour effects. More puzzling is the result of wearing a variety of materials when triplicating leg-covering: 'besides his ordinary stockings of silk, he wore under bootes another paire of woolen or wosted, with a paire of high linen boothose.' (1599).

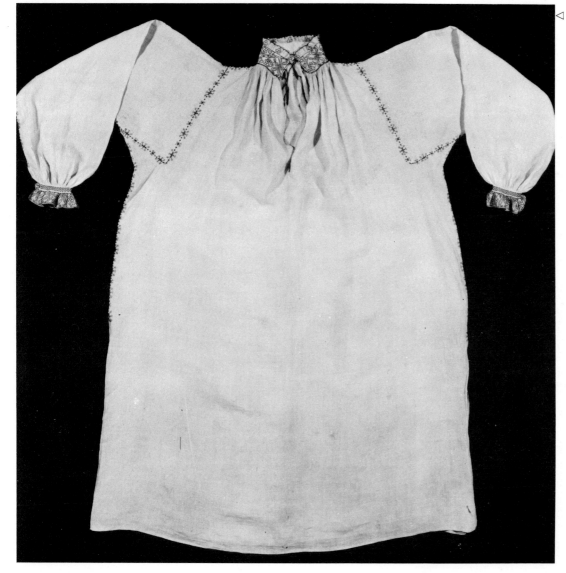

◁ Tudor man's linen shirt

Wrapped up from birth

Tudor babies began life so tightly rolled up in swaddling bands that scarcely a breath of air could reach the body.

At the age of seven or eight there was often a special family ceremony at which a boy was 'breeched'. Look at the portrait of Sir Walter Raleigh's son dressed like his father. He must have hated his baggy breeches, but those small boys who were the possessors of miniature dagger-proof, leather jerkins would have been very proud.

The picture on the right shows such a leather jerkin; it is an exact replica of an adult model, and is on view in the Museum of London.

The two pictures below right show two small girls of five. The Tudor child is already stiffly attired like an adult woman. Do you prefer the outfit of the small girl of today?

△

Tudor babies in swaddling clothes. *Cholmondeley Sisters*, c.1600

▷

A boy's leather jerkin, late sixteenth century

◁ Sir Walter Raleigh and his son

A five year old girl, 1590 ▷

Pictured right is a thick, knitted woollen vest for a Tudor child. Turn back to pages 34 and 35. What did adults wear next to the skin?

A Tudor child's vest ▷

The amusing extract below is from a description written in 1568 of boys being prepared for school. Note how many layers they were expected to wear over their vests.

The parent, unaware at first of the weather asks, 'Why have you taken your waistcoats? Is it so colde?. . .' and on finding that it is cold, 'Button your doublet. Where is your jerkin for this morning is somewhat colde and also take your coate' (worn over the jerkin). 'Take your perfumed gloves that are lined. Put on your gownes until we go and then we shall take your cloakes lyned with taffeta . . . Well, take your booten hosen!'

◁ The young Edward VI

The portrait on the left shows Henry VIII's son, Edward VI. Look up his dates on the chart at the end of this book.
Note his dagger and short upper hose. He has a doublet, which is like a jerkin but sleeved. Underneath, he wears a shirt and over his doublet a short gown – both like father's! He is wearing a hat indoors. Turn back to page 3. What were the dates of the two paintings? When you reach page 41, if you have not already guessed the reason, you will realise why people were beginning to wear less indoors in the late sixteenth century.

Make a list of what you wear summer and winter, inside and outside the house.

Tudor children might take off some garments outside in summer and then put them on again in the house. Can you suggest the reason?

Muffled up with no gaps

Look at the Queen in a pack of playing cards. The picture originates in the portrait of Henry VII's Queen, Elizabeth of York. Her large hood protected her from any draughts! Women often lodged their hoods, and later hats, on top of a close-fitting cap. Headgear was even worn for meals and dancing. For the less well-to-do, a nightcap often served for daytime as well as night. 'A knit night-cap made of coarsest twine with two long labels buttoned to his chin, rides he mounted on the market day.' (1581)

Elizabeth of York
▽

Gloves were carried for show but muffs kept the hands warm in winter.

You may see pictures of women in Tudor times with bare necks. However, head-dresses usually had long flaps. There are also many references to 'partlet-fill-ins' and 'chin clouts'. These suggest gaps could be closed whenever desired!

Large, loose garments lent themselves to linings. That most universal garment, the gown, was almost always lined as seen in the picture below right. The rich could afford sable. Rabbit skin was widely available. More economical was 'an old gowne faced with catts skynne' (1560). Women used a great variety of materials: velvet, silk, taffeta, damask, or fine wool. In 1535, Sir Owen Davidson left his nurse 'a gowne of satten lyned with velvet'.

Many women hitched up their gowns to reveal the lining. When the kirtle replaced the gown, the lining was usually stiffened, and when the wide skirt was displayed over the hooped frame of the farthingale, it was also lined.

English noblewoman, 1577
▽

When the circular cloak became a favourite
top garment for men this was splendidly
lined and every opportunity was taken to
show it off. The lining was often more
brilliant than the outside.

Long cloaks for travelling were usually
fur-lined for both men and women.
Waistcoats were commonly quilted inside.
Even stockings were sometimes lined.
Mention is made of 'a payer of round hose of
watchet kersey lined with bayes . . .'.

How many of your garments are lined?

The Elizabethan woman below, depicted by a
Flemish visitor to England, has nothing
exposed to the air except her eyes and nose.
Even her mouth is covered by a scarf!

The Tudor woollen cap in the picture on the
right has large flaps to cover up the ears. Men
sometimes tied these flaps underneath the
chin to prevent the wind blowing them away.
You can see this one in the Museum of
London.

A Tudor man's woollen ▷
cap

Edward VI, wearing a
richly-lined cloak
▽

EDWARD VI.
King of England.
Crowned 1547.
Born 1538.   Died 1553.

Tudor countrywoman,
1574 △

Tudor homes – a clue to Tudor costume?

Why can many people today wear thin clothing indoors even in winter?

Do you take off your coat in the house? Do your family wear hoods, caps or hats at meals? How is your home heated? Are some rooms much warmer than others? Is this the result of low ceilings; lack of draughts; double-glazing; insulation?

The reign of Henry VII followed a period of civil war. Many households were still living in damaged castles or buildings in bad repair. How could families keep warm in winter?

Henry VIII seized abbeys and monasteries and sold them to families who converted them to country homes. You needed to be tough to live in these rambling buildings. Think how medieval monks were clothed.

Buckland Abbey, Devon

A great burst of house building took place in the reign of Elizabeth I.

Longleat House was built between 1566 and 1580. Look at the picture below and try to count the number of large windows! How do you think the owners kept the house warm?

You can visit Buckland Abbey, built in Devon in the thirteenth century, and Longleat House in Wiltshire.

Longleat House, Wiltshire

40

In the reign of Elizabeth I, householders began to add chimneys to their homes, and they were installed in the large number of new houses constructed.

A chronicler writing early in her reign recalls: 'There are old men yet dwelling in the village where I remaine, which have noted three things within their sound remembrance. One is the multitudes of chimnies latilie erected, whereas in their young daies there were not above two or three if so many in most uplandish townes of the realme . . .'

Moreton Hall, Cheshire, a substantial house built in the reign of Elizabeth I, was constructed with only one original chimney stack. Huge galleries in the upper floors of homes like Montacute House, Somerset, were as cold as the open air, if not colder. The result was that caps continued to be needed indoors. Nor was it considered rude for a man, like the gentleman below, to wear his hat inside.

Yet habits were changing. In those rooms which were heated, wraps could be removed and headgear abandoned.

Did you guess the answer to the question about the difference between the heads of the two families in the pictures on page 3? The present world fuel shortage may mean a reduction of heat in twentieth-century homes!

Draw a cartoon of how your family might dress, or describe what you would wear, if you had little or no heat in your home.

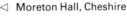

◁ Moreton Hall, Cheshire

A portrait of a Tudor gentleman, 1587

▽

Homes were not the only cold places

How is your school heated? What is the temperature in your classroom?

Look at the picture of a Tudor classroom, top right. Compare the large, unheated room, where the pupils were taught, with that of your classroom. How do you think the pupils were able to write in freezing weather?

Try to find out the temperature in a large shop, an office, or a room where committee meetings are held.

△ A Tudor classroom

A contemporary classroom ▷

◁ A meeting of the Court of Wards and Liveries during the reign of Elizabeth I

The picture on the left shows a meeting of some of the most important and wealthy men in the reign of Elizabeth I. There is no suggestion that the room in which they are gathered was heated. On the contrary, they are all muffled up and most of them are wearing hats. If you look closely you will see that near the top of the table is a 'hand-warmer'. This table-brazier was a new gadget introduced from Spain in the 1560s. Presumably, when someone wished to write he was able to thaw out his fingers!

The Bishop's Palace, St David's, Pembrokeshire

In the first half of the Tudor period a large part of the population had occupations connected with the church. The whole population attended church services on Sundays. Parish churches were usually built of stone or flint and had no heating. Monasteries, abbeys and priories usually had one warming room where their inmates were allowed to spend a brief period each day. Even a bishop's palace, like the one at St David's in Pembrokeshire pictured above, must have been a cold, rambling structure. Open fires were the only form of heat in the Tudor period. Can you spot any chimneys (do not be confused by the pinnacles) in the Palace at St David's?

The picture on the right shows an underground store designed to keep wool at an even temperature. It looks as if it must have been a chill, damp workplace for those who had to sort and stack the wool. Only in recent times have laws been passed controlling the temperature and humidity of places of work. Even today, not all factories are comfortable or healthy places to work. Most Tudor merchants would have been more worried about their materials than their workers.

A Tudor workplace: an underground wool store

An open-air life

Today, most people in Britain work indoors. There is a great variety of clothing, chosen to suit their occupations.

Even those who work outside on farms are rarely exposed to wind and rain. Look at the enclosed cab of the farm tractor in the picture.

Most of the population in Tudor times worked in the open air – the majority on the land or in occupations linked with farming. They were exposed to extremes of heat and cold, wind and dampness. It was important to try to keep warm and dry. They had little in the way of 'best clothes' until late Elizabethan times. Most of the pictures we can see of Tudor costume show wealthy ladies and gentlemen. Portraits were too expensive for the poor and there were no cameras in sixteenth-century England. We have to hunt for small drawings of people in working clothes. The kind of garments worn had changed little for several centuries. They were made from the materials most readily available and to meet practical needs.

A ploughman and his mate, c.1525

Above is a picture of a woman on her knees, milking a cow. She has a close-fitting hood which extends over her shoulders. She appears to be rolled in layers of clothing!

On the left is a picture of a ploughman and his mate. No warm tractor-cab for them! Both have their heads covered. They wear thigh-length jerkins opening at the front, which can either accommodate extra garments beneath or be easily discarded in heat. Most important is the amount of covering on their legs and their large, strong boots.

△

The Prime Minister on
her way to Parliament in
1979

Elizabeth I's chief
minister travelling in the
summer

▷

If you travelled in Tudor times, whether for
work or pleasure, whether you were rich or
poor, you had to wrap up to prepare for the
worst. Whatever means of transport used,
journeys were slow and the English weather
was no less liable to sudden changes than
it is today.

The picture above right shows William Cecil,
the most important minister of Queen
Elizabeth I, travelling in summertime. He is
covered up from top to toe and rides a small
pony.

Today the Prime Minister would travel in a
heated car and not even need to wear an
overcoat in winter. Most of us are
accustomed to heated, sometimes
over-heated, cars and trains.

Horse-drawn coaches had come into use on
the continent of Europe before the middle of
the sixteenth century. Queen Mary Tudor is
said to have owned the first one in England.
Elizabeth I ordered a state coach in 1564. It
was very draughty and little less bumpy than
a carter's waggon. She complained bitterly of
bruises. The picture on the right shows the
Queen in her coach on the way to the Palace
of Nonsuch in Surrey. It is not surprising she
preferred to travel on horseback.

Coaches carrying
Elizabeth I to her Palace
of Nonsuch

▽

Off to work. . .

Most people in Tudor times did not have far to travel to work. This was fortunate, for the only way to go, for the majority of workers, was on foot, like the construction engineers in the picture below. Notice how warmly clad and well shod they are. It is not surprising that there is such a large collection of worn-out sixteenth-century shoes at the Museum of London.

Shoes were often padded with moss for extra warmth.

Today a doctor would receive his patients in a warm surgery or visit the sick in a heated car. In Tudor times, a physician would often make his round of visits on foot. The physician in the picture on the right has doubled up on his headgear! He wears a long, loose, lined overcoat, known as a gabardine. He certainly has guarded himself against the colds he is setting out to cure!

A Tudor physician, 1562
▽

Surfeyte, age, and ſickenes, are enemyes all to health,
Medicines to mende the body excell all worldly wealth:
Piſicke ſhall floriſhe, and in daunger will giue cure,
Till death vnknit the liueſ knot no longer wee endure.

Tudor construction engineers
▽

The Tudors frequently travelled by water. To go to sea in a ship was the ambition of many sixteenth-century boys. Below right is our only surviving picture of an Elizabethan sailor. (Turn back to page 7 to remind yourself how we hope to discover more about clothes worn by Tudor sailors.) Note the jerkin and bags worn by the sailor. They were loose enough to allow for many layers of clothing beneath, which were probably never removed. Many seamen would be employed in the coastal traffic, which was far more extensive than today. Large rivers, like the Thames, were as busy as roads in Tudor times. Look at the number of craft shown on the river in the map on page 48.

The most famous journey by land in England in Tudor times is that of the actor, William Kemp, who jigged the 116 miles from London to Norwich in nine days. It was February and the ground was covered in snow. The outfit he is wearing may seem to contradict what has been said about the Tudors wrapping up. However, since he danced ten miles in three hours he scarcely needed a gabardine to keep him warm!

William Kemp jigging from London to Norwich, 1600
▽

A sailor, late sixteenth century   ▷

K emps nine daies vvonder.

Performed in a daunce from London to Norwich.

Containing the pleasure, paines and kinde entertainment of William Kemp betweene London and that Citty in his late Morrice.

Wherein is somewhat set downe worth note; to reprooue the slaunders spred of him: many things merry, nothing hurtfull.

Written by himselfe to satisfie his friends.

LONDON
Printed by E. A. for Nicholas Ling, and are to be solde at his shop at the west doore of Saint Paules Church. 1600.

The map below shows London when Queen Elizabeth I ascended the throne. It confirms many of the suggestions made in this book. The artist has illustrated the largest town in England, yet what strikes you about the scene? How close to the centre the fields extend! The town population was not divorced from country life. Most of the streets are too narrow for coaches. It is the river which is full of traffic. Although it is summertime, notice how the people in the foreground are well covered with clothing.

Remember that the Tudors lived in homes where you could not switch on electric fires if the evening turned cold. Churches and public buildings struck chill into the body even on hot days. People travelled by means which exposed them to draughts or sudden showers. Even in towns most of them worked in the open or in premises colder than the air outside. Beyond the town, one had to be prepared to meet every change in the notoriously unreliable English weather.

Think now about the way we dress today. Look at the list you made of the garments you wear.

What clues do our clothes give to the kind of life we lead today?

What seem to you the most striking differences between life today and life in Tudor times?

Elizabethan London
▽